Original title:
Snow-Flecked Daydreams

Copyright © 2024 Creative Arts Management OÜ
All rights reserved.

Author: Rory Fitzgerald
ISBN HARDBACK: 978-9916-94-494-3
ISBN PAPERBACK: 978-9916-94-495-0

Echoes of Stillness in a Frozen Realm

In the frosty air, a cow's dressed in style,
Bells on its collar, trots with a smile.
Penguins on ice, slipping and sliding,
Laughing so hard, it's joy they're providing.

Chickens in mittens, strutting about,
Dancing in circles, without any doubt.
Snowmen with sunglasses, looking so cool,
Making a snowball fight, the town's new rule.

A squirrel in goggles, ready to race,
Chasing his tail in the wintry space.
Trees wearing scarves, don't want to freeze,
Whispering secrets with each playful breeze.

Fluffy white flakes like popcorn in flight,
Kids try to catch them, what a silly sight!
With giggles that echo, they tumble around,
In this wacky world, pure laughter is found.

Beneath the Winter Veil

Beneath a veil so white and bright,
The snowmen dance, what a silly sight!
One has a carrot, the other a cup,
They stagger and wobble, they just can't stand up.

Pine trees wear hats of fluffy sheen,
While squirrels drop acorns and giggle unseen.
The snowflakes tumble, they put on a show,
If only they knew, they'd be late for the snow.

Lullabies of Icy Whirls

As snowflakes twirl in the chilly breeze,
A penguin salsa dances with ease.
He slips and he slides, what a comical scene,
Wearing a top hat, he looks quite the king.

The frost whispers secrets to frozen streams,
While ice cubes chatter and spin in their dreams.
A chorus of chuckles travels through air,
As winter's soft laughter fills everywhere.

Treading on Diamond Dreams

We tread on diamonds, oh what a treat,
With each step cracking, like candy to eat.
Fluffy paw prints of critters abound,
Oh, the joy in the mischief they found!

Hot cocoa spills as we march with cheer,
With marshmallows shouting, "We're also here!"
Giggling snowflakes join in the fun,
A whimsical party, and we've just begun!

Celestial Flurries of Hope

Chasing the flakes that swirl and glide,
A rabbit hops, with a giddy stride.
He wears a scarf, too big for his neck,
And tumbles around like a flying speck.

The stars twinkle down, with a wink and a grin,
Wishing the snowmen some luck to begin.
A chorus erupts from the chilly white haze,
With each snowy giggle, the whole world will blaze.

Impressions of Frost on a Dreaming Heart

In the frosty air, ducks wear hats,
While snowflakes dance like playful cats.
A mitten lost beneath the tree,
Giggles echo, wild and free.

Sleds run low with giggling glee,
Ice skates whisper tales of tea.
A snowman waves with button eyes,
While cheeky squirrels plot their heists.

Crystal Dreams on the Edge of Winter

Icicles glisten like shiny teeth,
Elves hide under the pine tree sheath.
Frosty breath turns into a plume,
As dogs run past with much to groom.

Soft flakes fall like powdered sugar,
A million giggles dance in their vigor.
With hats too big, and socks on hand,
We tumble down in the frosty land.

Secrets in the Drift of Cold Memories

Snowmen gossip beneath the stars,
While children throw snow like sweet guitars.
With noses red and cheeks aglow,
Our laughter rings in shimmering flow.

Cold feet dance on frozen lakes,
While hot cocoa warms the rambunctious wakes.
As winter's secrets start to unfold,
We trade warmth for stories bold.

Gleaming Whispers Under the Winter's Breath

Frosty fairies ride on a broom,
Stirring giggles throughout the gloom.
A snowball fight with cheerful screams,
In the quiet, mischief gleams.

Pine-scented dreams swirl in the night,
While shadows slip from the morning light.
With candy canes and fruity snacks,
We craft our joy, no looking back.

Dancing Shadows of Winter's Core

In a world where frost can dance,
Even penguins join the prance.
Each snowball flies with giggles loud,
As icicles form a chilly crowd.

Chasing flakes like furry mice,
Winter's chill? It feels so nice!
While snowmen share their silly grins,
They raise their hats, let the fun begin!

Frost-bitten toes in winter's game,
Sledding down, we feel no shame.
With every tumble, laughter bursts,
Creating memories, oh how it thirsts!

A snowman trip, a scarf askew,
Who knew winter was such a zoo?
As shadows dance in twilight's glow,
We twirl around with cheeks aglow.

Echoing the Cold's Caress.

The winter winds so slyly tease,
Whispers drift on frosty breeze.
Furry hats with silly ears,
Muffin mitts hold cups of cheers.

With every snowflake, laughter lands,
Making castles with frosty hands.
Sleds crash down in joyful heaps,
For winter fun, the laughter leaps.

Snowflakes fall like candy sprinkles,
Tickling noses, making crinkles.
Frosty breath in swirling clouds,
Cheerful yells from chilly crowds.

A chill doesn't mean we must frown,
Let's joyfully tumble down and down.
Life's a dance, a winter spree,
As we embrace this frosty glee!

Winter Whispers of Tomorrow

Whirlwinds spin with playful grace,
Chasing shadows in the race.
Jackets zipped to our chins,
A day of laughs, let's see who wins!

The crunching sound beneath our feet,
Frosty paths are quite the treat.
With every slip and tumble down,
We wear our grins like a crown.

Laughter echoes through the trees,
Frosty kisses on the breeze.
Giggling friends with rosy cheeks,
Winter's magic, oh how it peaks!

Snowflakes on our tongues, a game,
Every bite feels just the same.
With joy we gather, play and roam,
In winter's chill, we find our home.

Crystal-Covered Reveries

Dreams adrift on winter's play,
Glittering lights in bright display.
Gather 'round for stories told,
With every chuckle, warmth unfolds.

A plump bird perches, watching near,
Sneaky squirrels ignite our cheer.
In their chase, we laugh and run,
Winter mornings are simply fun.

Every flake with tales to share,
Is it magic or just a dare?
With mittens mixed, all colors bright,
We sculpt our world in pure delight.

A snowy scene where giggles bloom,
Giant leaps cause joyous boom.
With winter's charm that we adore,
Endless laughter, forevermore.

Chasing Shadows on a Powdered Path

In a world of white, I trip and slide,
Chasing shadows, my balance defied.
Penguins in suits, they laugh at my fall,
While I wiggle and dance, like a puppet ball.

Snowballs are missiles, I take aim with a grin,
But my aim is so bad, they just bounce off kin.
Laughter erupts, and I join in the cheer,
On this powdered path, the fun's crystal clear.

Frozen Echoes of Past Reflections

I glance in the mirror, an icicle beard,
Who knew winter could make me look weird?
A snowman beside me, gives me a wink,
Says, 'Hey buddy, it's time for a drink!'

In frozen rivers, my past self does skate,
Spinning and falling, oh, what a fate!
Echoes of laughter, they ring in my head,
While I roll in the snow, all covered in red.

Whirling Winds and Wandering Thoughts

Whirling winds tease my floppy old hat,
A chase through the air, oh what's up with that?
Thoughts drift away like snowflakes in flight,
Each one a giggle, oh what a delight!

A tumbleweed rolls, with a mind of its own,
I chase it, I giggle, my laughter has grown.
These wandering thoughts, they dance to the tune,
Of frosty fun days and a silly cartoon.

Icicle Visions Breathing Quiet Solace

Icicles hang like chattering teeth,
They speak of the winter, with no sign of grief.
Their glistening shapes, oh what a sight,
As they drip down like tears, in the light.

In cozy corners, I sip my hot drink,
While the world outside starts to shimmer and wink.
Quiet solace found in the freeze of the day,
Funny how laughter still finds its own way.

Whispered Hopes Amidst Silvery Flurries

Tiny flakes fall, a frosty dance,
They tickle my nose, give giggles a chance.
Laughter erupts as I trip on my feet,
Playing hopscotch in the cold, such a treat!

The world is a canvas, painted in white,
My mittened hands sculpt snowballs with delight.
They soar through the air, a flight of pure glee,
But oops, now my cat's the target, oh dear me!

Luminescent Shadows in the Winter's Gloom

The sun peeks out, a shy little beam,
It sparkles on frost like a glistening dream.
Snowmen dance with a vibrant flair,
One loses a hat—oh, how he does stare!

In the chilly air, the children run wild,
Their cheeks painted pink, every grown-up a child.
A snowball parade, right into my coat,
With squeals of pure joy, they're all in remote.

Dreams Adorned with Ice-Covered Jewels

Icicles dangle, a chandelier tease,
While penguins on sleds slide past with such ease.
Hot cocoa in hand, it spills on my chin,
I lick off the mess; oh, where to begin?

Frosted delights make me giggle and grin,
The mailman waves back—he's got snow on his skin!
With marshmallows plopped like a frosty crown,
Who knew winter fun could turn upside down?

Quiet Moments in a Blustery Reverie

There's a calm in the storm that's oddly amusing,
When snowflakes conspire and start to be choosing.
I watch little critters with fluffy round tails,
Sledding on pinecones, oh, how the laughter trails!

The wind whispers secrets, like giggles in flight,
As two snowmen wave with carrots held tight.
In this winter's wonder, with hearts big and bright,
Every blustery moment brings pure sheer delight!

Glistening Threads of Dream's Design

In a world of frozen fluff,
Twirling penguins dance in a puff.
Sipping cocoa, I might scatter,
Marshmallows on my head, oh what a clatter!

Chanting snowmen sing in the park,
Belly flops leave an indelible mark.
Glistening threads of giggles bright,
Wrap us snug in fuzzy delight.

With playful nips from frostbite's teeth,
We chase our laughter, so sweet beneath.
A carrot nose, not quite on right,
Just adds to the silly, merry night.

So let us dream with gleeful cheer,
With hats askew, we've nothing to fear.
In this land where chuckles gleam,
We weave and we wander in silly dream.

Shimmering Thoughts in the Icy Afterglow

Glittering ice, a magical sheen,
Skating penguins wear a silly green.
In this wintery world full of zest,
Cold noses frolic, ice-blocks at rest.

With snowflakes swirling, tickling toes,
Laughter rises where no one knows.
Waddling about, we trip with glee,
Frosty laughter, a wild jubilee.

Hot chocolate rivers, a syrupy stream,
Swirling as I drift, in a sweet dream.
A marshmallow snowman takes a dive,
Making us laugh, makes us feel alive!

Shimmering thoughts drift up on high,
Like jolly whispers that waltz and fly.
In this chilly, gleeful embrace,
We find our joy in this frosted place.

Snowy Delusions in the Heart of Winter

Dancing snowflakes in all their glory,
Bunnies hop with a giggling story.
Ice cream cones with snow on top,
Oh, silly visions that just won't stop!

Fluffy kittens in winter's bliss,
Chasing their tails with a frosty hiss.
Jolly snowmen sport wacky hats,
And all the world just stops and chats.

With each frosty breath, we huff and puff,
Claiming winter's chill is never too tough.
In our frosty, whimsical play,
The heart of winter becomes our stage.

So let's toast marshmallows under the sun,
Crafting snowmen, one by one.
With delusions wrapped in laughter's embrace,
We dance through the snow with a silly grace.

Hallowed Dreams Under a Frosted Moon

Under a moon that gleams and glows,
The trees wear coats of ice like pros.
Frosty whispers swirl through the night,
As giggles sparkle in wintry light.

With snowball fights that might go awry,
We see the snowmen take to the sky.
Waving their twiggy arms with delight,
They dive and roll, what a silly sight!

Hallowed dreams dance in crisp air,
Chasing each other without a care.
We flutter like snowflakes, light and free,
In a sparkly world of titter and glee.

So gather 'round, let laughter reign,
In this frosty wonderland, nothing is plain.
With hearts aglow under the moon's wise watch,
We'll carve snowy tales, each a delightful notch!

Glistening Thoughts on a Frigid Landscape

Dancing flakes paint the ground bright,
Hats are slipping, what a sight!
Frosty noses and icy toes,
Can't feel my fingers, where'd they go?

Sleds are stuck on a hefty slope,
Chasing laughter, we grip and grope.
Snowmen sag with a carrot nose,
Wobbly forms in winter clothes.

Hot cocoa spills with laughter loud,
Mittens swap, we join the crowd.
Giggles echo through the freeze,
It's a riot, just like a breeze.

Pine trees wear their snowy caps,
Boys and girls take joyous laps.
Snowball fights, a playful stew,
Oh, winter, how we play in you!

Enigma Encased in Winter Light

Beneath a cloak of white delight,
We tumble down from silly heights.
A snowman blinks with button eyes,
Did he see me eat those pies?

The igloo stands, but it's quite small,
Laughter pings off every wall.
Inside, we sip from frosty mugs,
Outside, we race like playful bugs.

Fluffy creatures, all around,
Snowdrifts high, we leap and bound.
Snowflakes tickle, laughter's near,
Even squirrels crack a cheer.

Gloves make mittens; oh, what fun!
Chasing snowflakes, one by one.
Winter wonder, wrapped so tight,
In this laughter, everything's bright.

Dreamscapes of the Bitter Chill

Shivers dance along the street,
Frozen footsteps, skip-a-beat.
Frosty breath becomes a cloud,
Achoo! That sneeze; it's winter loud!

Ice slides gleam, oh what a show,
Wipe out laughs in the fresh snow.
Cramming snowballs, laughter swirls,
Madly we toss, we're tangled girls.

Pigeons wear their copious fluff,
Are they laughing? This is tough!
A sudden slip, a screeching shout,
Who knew winter would bring this bout?

Laughter rings while cold winds blow,
Winter dances, we lose our glow.
In this chill, our hearts ignite,
Funny tales frame the winter night.

A Canvas of Ice and Imagination

What's this? A canvas, oh so bright,
Little hands bring dreams to light.
Snowflakes sprinkle, giggles soar,
In this frosty world, we want more!

Sleds whiz past with squeaky glee,
Round and round, just you and me.
Twinkling lights on rooftops shine,
Oh, how this winter feels divine!

Chattering teeth and rosy cheeks,
In the snow, we chase, we sneak.
Whoops! A falls, and laughter flies,
We tumble like snowballs, oh so spry!

At night we gather, stories shared,
Chilly jests, no one's scared.
Under stars, our dreams expand,
Laughing hearts, united stand!

Icy Echoes of a Tranquil Mind

In winter's clutch, my thoughts take flight,
With snowballs tossed, in pure delight.
A penguin slides, quite out of place,
As I sip cocoa, in a dreamy haze.

The squirrels wear tiny knit caps,
While I hear laughter of the snowmap traps.
I chuckle as icicles drop with a clang,
Nature's own joke, the ice-cold twang.

Flurries of Solitude and Wonder

A snowman stands with a crooked nose,
His carrot's lost under a pile of snows.
I wave to him, he tips his hat,
Drunk on frosty tips from a snowy spat.

The flakes are dancing, a frosty ballet,
While warm socks hug my feet, oh, what a play!
Birds wear mittens, and I burst in cheer,
Who knew winter could tickle my ear?

Silent Soliloquies in White

The frost bites gently, a ticklish spree,
While hidden snow thieves tattoo the tree.
I shudder and giggle at the whispers so sly,
As marshmallows tumble right out of the sky.

The trees wear frosty coats that gleam,
While I chase my thoughts like a frosty dream.
A snowball miss lands right on my shoe,
And suddenly winter is giggling too.

Enchanted Dreams Under a Frosty Veil

The snowflakes dance like clowns in the air,
Each one unique, a wonder to share.
My cat plots mischief in the frosty glow,
As I sip from mugs shaped like a snowman's toe.

With frosted whispers and giggles of light,
I dream of giants in pajamas at night.
A toasty sock fights a chilly breeze,
And laughter rings out 'neath the evergreen trees.

Whispers of Frosted Reverie

In the chilly air, I spot a hare,
Wearing a scarf, with quite a flair.
He hops and skips, with such delight,
Dancing on ice, a comical sight.

A snowman grins, with a carrot nose,
Telling bad jokes in frozen prose.
His snowball jokes, they fall quite flat,
But still we laugh, at his silly spat.

Penguins in suits, so dapper and sleek,
Waddle and slide, as they play hide and seek.
They trip and tumble, with flapping arms,
In this frosty world, they have their charms.

As snowflakes twirl, in a wild ballet,
Clouds giggle softly, in a cloud-like way.
We dream of mischief in winter's embrace,
In this chilly wonder, we find our grace.

Winter's Glistening Mirage

There's a giant bear, sipping hot tea,
With polar friends, a sight to see.
They dress in sweaters, oh so bright,
Laughing at rhymes, with pure delight.

Icicles shine like silly hats,
Hanging from roofs, like frozen bats.
The squirrels chatter, plotting a scheme,
To steal the birdseed, oh what a dream.

Frosty fingers wave, in the breeze,
Tickling cheeks, with such frosty tease.
They poke at noses, and giggle just right,
As we chase snowflakes, dancing in flight.

In this wonderland where laughter flows,
Every snowdrift hides a joke, who knows?
We find pure joy, in this winter's tale,
With chuckles and cheer, we shall prevail.

Chasing Crystal Fantasies

On a shimmering lake, a rabbit sails,
In a tiny boat, with paper trails.
He shouts out, 'Look! I'm a captain bold!'
As fish swim by, with secrets untold.

Chickadees chat, while dressed in white,
Trying to sing, but getting it right.
They chirp out tunes, then switch to dance,
In this frosty world, we take a chance.

Fluffy clouds join, in the winter fun,
Making funny shapes, under the sun.
A dog in goggles, chasing a kite,
Laughing in circles, such pure delight.

And as we wander, through sparkly glows,
Each step we take, the laughter just grows.
In this magical land of frosty play,
Every moment glimmers, in a funny way.

Frosted Fantasia at Dawn

Awakening gently, to a world of fluff,
In pajamas warm, we bundle up tough.
A snowball fight, oh what a spree,
With giggles and laughter, such pure glee.

A silly snowdog, with floppy ears,
Fetches a snowball, and brings it near.
But wait! It's a carrot, not quite right,
He pouts and snorts, what a funny sight.

Old boots parade, with holes galore,
Slipping and sliding across the floor.
They squeak and squawk, like happy ducks,
In this frosty morning, we share our lucks.

So here's to whimsy, on frosted ground,
As frolicking spirits of charm abound.
We'll laugh and play, till the daylight fades,
In a winter world, where joy cascades.

When the World Turns to Silver

A blizzard of giggles, it sweeps through the street,
Where snowmen wear hats made of leftover meat.
Children throw snowballs, it's a comical fight,
While penguins in bow ties join the sheer delight.

Sleds zooming fast, a race through the park,
One dog steals the toboggan, oh what a lark!
Everyone's laughing, slipping and sliding,
As snowflakes are landing, the joy is colliding.

Hot cocoa's served with marshmallow fluff,
One sip and you'll know, it's ridiculously tough!
The snowflakes are giggling as they dance on the eaves,
While frostbitten noses play tricks on our sleeves.

And when night falls softly like a fluffy old quilt,
We wonder whose cake was stolen and spilt?
With a wink and a chuckle, the moon gives a glance,
As we twirl through the chaos—what a winter dance!

Frosted Illusions Beneath the Stars

Under a quilt of frost, dreams wander and sway,
A squirrel in a tutu with ballet on display.
Jacketed penguins applaud from the side,
While marshmallow clouds set the stage for the ride.

Frosty cupcakes shrink under stars' mighty heat,
A snowman declares them the best kind of treat.
Laughter erupts from a cat in a hat,
As it twirls through the drifts, looking sleek and quite fat.

Icicles dangle like bling from above,
While snowflakes are falling, all twinkling with love.
And the moonlight, it chuckles, lighting up the night,
As we slip on the ice, what a comical sight!

So gather your dreams on this chilly parade,
With snowflakes to toss, let the fun be displayed.
Under the stars, where laughter runs wild,
We cherish the moments, the jester, the child.

Glacial Hues of Remembrance

In a world painted blue, with laughter in tow,
Two snowflakes gossip, wandering to and fro.
A penguin with glasses reads tales from a book,
While a polar bear dances—oh, come take a look!

Frosted footprints lead to a disco ball tree,
With disco balls twirling, we're merry as can be.
The laughter runs rampant, like bubbles in air,
As we join in the fun, with glitter to spare.

Snowmen are arguing, who wears the best coat,
While flurries keep giggling, in snowdrifts they float.
And icicles chime softly, like bells on the breeze,
As snowball fights break out with the greatest of ease.

So if you should wander on this glacial spree,
Remember the laughter that dances in glee.
For every cold moment brings warmth when it's shared,
With snowflakes as witnesses, forever ensnared.

The Enchanted Chill of Twilight

Twilight drapes softly with a shimmer and twirl,
As snowflakes take flight, all frosty and swirl.
A rabbit in shades sips hot chocolate divine,
While squirrels in tuxedos toast under moonshine.

With penguins as waiters and snowballs to serve,
A laughing parade takes a wintery swerve.
Jokes are exchanged as snowflakes convene,
In a world where the cold can't freeze all the keen.

Bubbles of laughter dance up to the moon,
As snow angels form with a comical swoon.
And the frost-covered trees wear hats made of light,
As we join in the joy of this enchanted night.

So come take a spin on this glittery floor,
Where each frosty moment asks for just one more.
In a chilly embrace, the fun never fades,
As we whirl through the twilight, in laughter cascades.

Enchanted Twilight in a Glacial Dreamscape

In a land where snowmen dance,
And penguins wear their finest pants,
Icicles drip like tipsy hats,
While rabbits hop in fuzzy flats.

Breezes play a frosty tune,
As polar bears chase after spoons,
Sledding down a cupcake hill,
Laughter echoes, time stands still.

Each flake is painted with a grin,
As bunnies spin like they're in sin,
Giggling snowflakes swirl around,
In this icy fun zone, joy is found.

As twilight fades, the stars appear,
They twinkle jokes we can all hear,
With each glistening, crafty gleam,
Life's a nonsensical, frosty dream.

Dreaming in the Frost-Laden Air

Fluffy clouds with hats of white,
Bounce around, what a delight!
With chilly giggles in the sky,
As snowmen joke, 'Oh my, oh my!'

Squirrels skate on frozen ponds,
While snowflakes play in endless bonds,
Hot cocoa rivers flow on by,
With marshmallow boats that never die.

The frozen trees wear coats of fluff,
As children shout, 'This is enough!'
With laughter ringing, hearts aglow,
In frost-laden air, we let it show.

Chasing visions on a slide,
With goofy grins we take the ride,
In this whimsical, frozen land,
Every moment's silly, nothing bland.

A Serenity Wrapped in Crystal Dreams

Glistening lies upon the ground,
With chubby cheeks, we spin around,
Frosty whispers in the night,
Telling tales of snowball fights.

Lollipops dangle from the trees,
As owls wear socks and dance with ease,
Nutty critters sing a tune,
Underneath the frosty moon.

Frosty hats and sparkly gloves,
Amidst the fun, we're filled with love,
Each chilly gust a gentle tease,
In crystal dreams, we find our keys.

With twinkling lights and gummy bears,
We tumble down the ice-cold stairs,
Wrapped in laughter, joy, and schemes,
As we drift on icy streams.

Whimsical Flights on Icy Wings

Butterflies made of ice and cheer,
Zigzagging angles, what a smear!
With floating games of dress-up fun,
Dressed as snowflakes, everyone.

Perched on trees are giggling birds,
Wearing coats of sandwich nerds,
They chirp a tune we all can hum,
About a world where sweets grow dumb.

Hopping bunnies in a play,
Hopscotch races through the gray,
Every leap brings silly glee,
In the air, we're wild and free.

With icy wings, we take our flight,
Through frosty skies, a swirling sight,
Together in this playful spree,
Soaring high, just you and me.

Frosted Mirth in the Midst of Solitude

In slippers warm, I dance around,
While snowmen chuckle, lost, and found.
A carrot nose, a woeful frown,
What's next? A snowball fight in town!

Hot cocoa spills, I sip too fast,
The marshmallows float, a frothy blast.
Did I just taste a snowman's hat?
Oh dear, my giggles start to splat!

The winter sun, a jester's grin,
I trip on ice, I spin, I win!
With frozen toes and laughter loud,
Alone, but happy at this shroud!

A snowflake lands upon my nose,
Tickling me, as winter flows.
The world is white, a funny show,
In solitude, I dance and glow!

Slumbering Wishes on a Winter Canvas

A blanket white, the lawn does snore,
Dreams of snowball fights galore.
But wait! My sled is stuck in goo,
I laugh so hard, a funny view!

With puffy coats, we brave the chill,
But then we slip, oh what a thrill!
Sledding down a hill, what a blast,
Oh no, we're stuck, and time goes fast!

A snow angel waves, flaps a wing,
"Join me here, you're free to swing!"
I flop about, a floundering fish,
"More cocoa, please, this is my wish!"

The chill creeps in, my toes turn numb,
Snowflakes tickle, feeling dumb.
Yet laughter crackles, fills the air,
In frozen dreams, we dance with flair!

Enchanted Echoes of the Frozen Woods

Deep in the trees where whispers glide,
My ski pole sinks, I take a ride.
An echo bounces back with glee,
"Who's there?" I shout, "It's just me!"

The branches shake, they giggle too,
A squirrel schemes, what will he do?
He leaps from branch, a frosty dart,
What a surprise, oh bless my heart!

With fluffy cheeks and frosty breath,
I tumble down with grace, but mess.
A deer observes, a frozen stare,
"Is this a dance? You should beware!"

Caught in a swirl of winter cheer,
Each fallen flake brings laughter near.
In snow-clad woods, in giggles hide,
Echoes of joy we can't abide!

Glistening Dreams in Crystal Casements

Through windows frosted, I gaze outside,
The world is bright, my thoughts collide.
A snowman's dancing, quite absurd,
I crack a smile, oh, what a word!

A frosty bird, in cap and tie,
Takes flight with flair, oh me, oh my!
I join the fun, can't help but laugh,
In winter's grip, we write our path!

With every flake like cotton spun,
I build a fortress, while we run.
A epic battle of snow and fun,
"Retreat!" I scream, but who has won?

With cheeks aglow and hands so cold,
Stories of winter beg to be told.
In crystal casements, dreams take wing,
A funny world, oh, let's all sing!

Tinkling Dreams Beneath the Hushed Sky

In clouds of cotton candy spun,
The world is laughing, just for fun.
A rabbit hops in boots of green,
With big blue shades, he's quite the scene,

The stars are winking, oh so bright,
Playing tag with the moon each night.
A squirrel juggles acorns with glee,
While giggles echo through the trees.

A snowman dreams on winter's stage,
Wearing a scarf that's all the rage.
His carrot nose, a silly sight,
Makes him the king of frosty night.

Beneath the hush, the world's a cheer,
With frosty giggles filling the air.
So let's embrace this playful bliss,
And dance in snowflakes, can't resist!

Blanketed Secrets of a Frosty Night

A penguin slips on icy ground,
With every tumble, laughter's found.
He wears a hat that's far too wide,
And tumbles down with joyful pride.

The trees are dressed in sparkling white,
As critters gather, what a sight!
They toast marshmallows on a twig,
While telling tales, both small and big.

Frosty giggles fill the air,
As snowflakes whirl without a care.
A hidden fox with icy toes,
Joins in the fun, as laughter grows.

A blanket thick, beneath the sky,
Where secrets dance, and snowflakes sigh.
In frosty fun, we chase the night,
With whispers soft, and hearts so light!

Wandering Wishes on a Frozen River

Upon the ice, we glide and sway,
With dreams as bright as Christmas Day.
A penguin skates with style unmatched,
While frosty giggles are attached.

The river sings a merry tune,
Under a sleepy, watching moon.
With each small slip, a chuckle flies,
As snowmen wink with frosted eyes.

A curious cat just cannot resist,
And hops right in with a snowy twist.
The fish below, they must be glad,
To see such antics—oh, it's rad!

Wishes wander on ice so wide,
With chilly breezes as our guide.
Let laughter reign, a joyful cheer,
As frosty dreams bring us near.

Whispers of Wonder in the Silent Snow

In gentle hush, the world unfolds,
With stories whispered, oh so bold.
The woodland critters gather round,
With silly hats and laughter found.

A bear in boots, dancing with flair,
While bunnies chuckle without a care.
A snowflake lands on a bunny's nose,
And giggles burst, as everyone knows.

The trees sway softly, their branches swing,
To frosty tunes that winter brings.
While woodland friends prepare a feast,
Of berry pies for all, at least!

Beneath the stars, a dreamer's glow,
With laughter ringing through the snow.
The night is young, with joy in tow,
As whispers dance, a frosty show!

Frosted Fantasies at Dusk

The snowman wore a silly hat,
With a carrot for a nose like that.
He danced around, jiggled with glee,
Singing tunes for all to see.

A rabbit joined with floppy ears,
Spinning tales of winter's cheers.
They frolicked under fading light,
Cheering up the cold, long night.

With snowballs flying here and there,
They threw them high, without a care.
Giggles echoed through the trees,
Hiding laughter in the breeze.

As stars twinkled, the night was bright,
A frozen party, pure delight.
In this fantasy, they'd always play,
Chasing cold blues far away.

Chilled Thoughts on a Silent Eve

A penguin slips, oh what a sight,
Waddling awkwardly, oh so light.
He twirls around, loses his grip,
And takes a frosty little trip.

The crows above squawk with disdain,
"Watch out below!" They cackle and feign.
But the penguin laughs in pure delight,
As everyone joins in for the night.

The icy air stirred with their cheer,
As snowflakes danced, crystal clear.
No worries, just carefree fun,
On this frozen eve, under the sun.

As the moon climbed high, the chill persisted,
With warm hearts, no one resisted.
They laughed and played until they'd tire,
In this winter's sweet, joyful choir.

Dreams Adrift in Winter's Embrace

The squirrel in his furry coat,
Jumps around, can hardly float.
He stashes acorns in the snow,
Dreams of summer's sun aglow.

The owl in the tree can't help but stare,
At this furry friend with little care.
With a hoot, the owl did say,
"Chill out, buddy! It's winter play!"

A fox sneaks in, quite the trickster,
With mischief dancing like a whisker.
They race beneath the glimmering sky,
In a wild chase of snowflakes high.

Laughter carried on the breeze,
Amongst the twinkles of frosty trees.
In these moments, they found delight,
In their simple dreams, pure and bright.

Frosty Lullabies Beneath the Stars

Beneath the blanket of night so deep,
Animals gather, not a sound, they leap.
The deer tiptoe, a graceful sight,
Singing softly to the chilly night.

A sleepy bear hums lullabies,
While snowflakes fall like twinkling eyes.
The chilly air fills up with cheer,
As winter's song drifts far and near.

The moon overhead, a watchful friend,
Winks at those who pretend to blend.
Together they sway, around they spin,
In frosty dreams where fun begins.

With each note, the night they charm,
Embracing cold without a qualm.
In this winter wonder, laughter bright,
Frosty lullabies fill the night.

Ephemeral Whispers on a Wintry Canvas

A frosty breeze with a teasing grin,
Tickles my nose, let the giggles begin.
Chasing snowflakes that look like confetti,
I trip on my boots, oh isn't it petty!

Frosty cats slide across the white ground,
With each wobbly step, laughter is found.
A penguin parade waddles so slow,
In this chilly chaos, I steal the show!

Hot cocoa spills, what a sweet little mess,
With marshmallows dancing, I must confess.
The world is a stage of this snowy delight,
Where whimsy and laughter twirl into night!

A snowman with hats stacked way too high,
Winks at the sun, as it kisses the sky.
In a world so crazy, full of quick quips,
Let's ride on this laughter, with icy licks.

A Dance of Frost Upon Dreaming Eyes

Icicles hang like decorations on trees,
Snowflakes pirouette in a chilly breeze.
The mittens I lost, oh where have they gone?
A frosty ballet where cold toes have shone!

My friend took a tumble, went head over heels,
While clutching a snowball, oh what great reels!
With noses all red and laughter in sight,
We tumble through snow, what a goofy flight!

Chattering teeth, I make silly faces,
While polar bears wonder about our wild chases.
Comical flurries in frost-covered cheer,
As giggles and grins bring warmth to the year!

In a snow globe of joy, we leap and we spin,
Making memories where the laughter begins.
With fun on our faces, all worries are tossed,
In a world of pure magic, we gain what we've lost.

Shards of Ice and Gentle Reverie

Crystal castles spark in the frosty light,
As I fumble my steps, oh what a sight!
My dog dons a sweater, looking quite grand,
In a fashion parade, he's the star of the land!

Laughter erupts as we stumble and giggle,
The ground beneath us starts bouncing and wiggle.
With cocoa mustaches and noses all red,
The joy in our hearts dances wide and spread!

A snowball flies, missed the mark, oh dear!
Heckles erupt, like music to my ear.
With every mishap, the comedy grows,
In this blizzard of bliss, anything goes!

Each shadowy figure holds secrets untold,
As we laugh in the winter, bright and bold.
No day is too dreary if laughter takes flight,
On a canvas of ice, bathed in soft light.

Ethereal Prayers in the Cold Light

Mittens lost somewhere, I'm on a quest,
Chasing after joy in this grand winter fest.
With snowflakes as pom-poms, we cheer and we shout,
A team of fluffy clouds, all dancing about!

Snowmen with faces that look quite confused,
Who knew that the snow would leave us bemused?
With carrots for noses, and buttons askew,
We laugh at their style, it's a fashion debut!

Fluffy bunnies hop with their hats on the run,
As we whirl 'round the trees, oh so much fun!
Chasing bright dreams through the chilly white haze,
We twirl in delight, our hearts all ablaze!

With shadows that stretch like silly old jokes,
The chill in the air gives life to the folks.
In the warmth of our chuckles, we banish the night,
Spinning frosty prayers in the soft morning light.

Ethereal Chills of Longing

In winter's grasp, we dance and twirl,
With laughter echoing, flags unfurl.
A snowman with a carrot nose,
Winks at us, while the cold wind blows.

Hot cocoa spilled on a frosty floor,
Mittens wrestling with a neighbor's dog,
"Snowball fight!"—but wait, oh no!
My best friend slipped in a cozy fog!

Chattering teeth, we scheme and plot,
To build a fort that hits the spot.
But first, we pause for a snowflake taste,
Catching them quick, with playful haste!

At dusk, the world becomes a scene,
Bright lights twinkling, glistening sheen.
The moon peeks down with a grin so wide,
In this snowy realm, let joy abide!

Glimmering Dreams Beneath a Blanket of White

Under layers of white, we find our cheer,
More than cold, it brings us near.
A sled goes flying, oh what a sight,
With giggles trailing into the night!

We fashion angels without a care,
Our mittens damp from the frosty air.
The world a canvas, we paint and play,
In glimmering joy, we'll seize the day!

A cat in boots, so proud and bold,
Chasing snowflakes, a sight to behold.
And much to our surprise, behold this fact,
The dog leapt high, then fell—how tact!

At evening's fall, we gather tight,
Telling tales 'round a firelight.
With marshmallows toasted, laughter rings,
In this frolicking dream, winter sings!

Frosted Petals in a Silent Garden

In a garden wrapped in crystal frost,
Petals shimmer, never lost.
A gnome with glasses, sitting askew,
Looks up and whispers, "Kind of you!"

The fairies dance on chilly leaves,
Twirling tales of their winter eves.
With snowflakes caught in their twinkling hair,
They giggle as they vanish in thin air.

We tiptoe past the frozen pond,
Where ducks play king, and the sunlight's fond.
"The ice could crack!" one friend exclaimed,
But the duck just preened, completely unashamed!

Beneath a blanket of still so bright,
Laughter echoes through the night.
Winter's embrace, a curious friend,
In frosted petals, we find the blend!

A Tapestry of Cold Reflections

Under a quilt of crystal fair,
Lies the world, without a care.
Reflections dance in the shining dew,
A troupe of giggles, all very true!

Icicles hang like swords of light,
While snowflakes swirl in dizzy flight.
A bear in shades strolls by with glee,
"Do you know how much I love this spree?"

A tree with branches all coated white,
Wears a hat of snow with pure delight.
"Twist and shout," we suddenly sing,
Around the yard, our joy takes wing!

As the sun dips low, we dance and prance,
In this frosty wonder, we take our chance.
For laughter echoes, like bells on high,
In a cold tapestry, we all comply!

Crystalized Visions in Winter's Grip

In a world of flakes that dance,
My thoughts take on a peculiar stance.
A penguin slips, a sight so bold,
I laugh till I can't feel the cold.

The icicles hang like chandeliers,
While snowmen dodge the frostbite fears.
A squirrel in boots, strutting about,
In snowball fights, it's full of clout.

Frosty fingers tickle the air,
I trip over mounds without a care.
With each tumble, giggles abound,
In this winter wonder, joy is found.

So here's to the whimsy on display,
Where frozen chuckles lead the way.
In a realm of laughter, pure and bright,
I find warmth in this chilly delight.

Etheral Frost and Transient Thoughts

Chasing flakes as they swirl around,
A yodeling snowman, what a sound!
With scarves that twist and giggle in glee,
I join the frolic, carefree as can be.

Slippery paths lead to unplanned bounds,
My brain does flips while my balance confounds.
An icy patch, a graceful pirouette,
Laughter erupts; this day I won't forget.

Santa's sleigh whizzes, but oh, watch out!
A reindeer in shorts makes me scream and shout.
The frozen giggles fill up the space,
As snowflakes join in the merry race.

In this frosty realm of absurd play,
My heart finds joy in the silliest way.
For each chilly mishap brings cheer,
In winter's embrace, I have nothing to fear.

Glacial Mirrors of the Soul

Reflections shimmer on the icy lake,
I see my face, and I start to shake!
A snow-covered hat goes flying by,
As I chase it, I can't help but cry.

Frozen fish with hats on their fins,
In this sweet madness, the giggling begins.
A polar bear doing the cha-cha slide,
This laugh-fest is something I won't hide.

The chill in the air brings frosty cheer,
Where nonsense reigns, and all's sincere.
Strangers become pals in this frosty mist,
Join in the fun; you simply can't resist!

With every slip and frosty fall,
We gather together, standing tall.
In this shimmering chill, we find a goal,
The warmth of laughter, the glacial soul.

Whirling Fantasies in the Icy Air

A flurry of thoughts, whizzing on by,
I tumble and spin, oh my, oh my!
With mittened hands red as a bright rose,
I'm dodging the snowballs, strikes, and throws.

Penguins in hats, what a sight to see!
Breakdancing on ice, so wild and free.
A snowflake zips past and buzzes my ear,
Whispering jokes that make me cheer.

With frosty fingers and toes a bit numb,
I chase after humor like children run.
A snow angel giggles, an echo so fine,
In this winter ballet, the fun intertwines.

So here in the cold, I jump and I play,
In the swirling white, I find my way.
With laughter and joy, this season is bright,
A whimsical dance in the frosty light!

Fragments of Fantasy in Winter's Fold

A penguin in a top hat struts,
While snowflakes tickle winter's guts.
The trees wear coats of fluffy white,
They giggle softly in delight.

A squirrel slides on icy rays,
Chasing dreams through frosty maze.
With cocoa spilling from a cup,
The world's a waltz, so lift it up!

Icicles form a silly grin,
As winter plays a cheeky spin.
The fox wears boots and laughs a tune,
While lazing under a snowy moon.

Chimneys puff like dragons brave,
Through crystal air, our laughter waves.
The season's charm, it swirls and spins,
In frosty games, let fun begin!

Polished Reflections of a Shimmering Mind

The mirror shows a penguin dance,
With fluffy feet that twist and prance.
A snowman sports a carrot nose,
As winter giggles, who knows where it goes?

Glistening skies in shades of mirth,
The sun holds ice cream for what it's worth.
While snowballs fly in comical arcs,
The laughter echoes through the parks.

A hare with glasses reads a book,
As frosty fairies steal a look.
With every page, the giggles flow,
In polished dreams where humor grows.

While arctic winds spin tall tales,
The frosty fun never fails.
We laugh aloud, with cheeks aglow,
In shiny dreams where silliness flows!

Secrets Wrapped in a Frosty Shroud

Beneath the snow, a rabbit snores,
Dreaming of candy-coated shores.
The flakes conspire with winter's chill,
A secret dance, but who will spill?

The wise old owl hoots with glee,
As mischief brews in every tree.
With frosty whispers, giggles rise,
In shrouded dreams where humor lies.

A polar bear with quirky hats,
Plays hide and seek amidst the spats.
In shimmering tricks, the laughter grows,
With secrets wrapped like frosted bows.

The wind howls jokes, both snarky and bright,
While dancing shadows bring pure delight.
In winter's hold, we chase the fun,
Where laughter thrives until we're done!

Chilled Dreams in a Glacial Realm

Giddy snowflakes tumble down,
Tickling noses in this town.
A penguin slips and makes a scene,
In dreamy frolics, oh so keen.

With every gust, the snowmen sway,
As fluffy clouds join in the play.
Lopsided grins and crooked hats,
Bring chuckles soft, like purring cats.

The ice rinks spark with laughter loud,
As everyone twirls, quite proud.
With fancy moves that bring a cheer,
Chilled dreams will dance throughout the year.

The winter's chill can't freeze our grin,
In glacial realms, let fun begin!
For in this world of white delight,
We find our joy, oh what a sight!

The Art of Frosted Wishes

A snowman wearing shades, so cool,
Stands proudly by the frozen pool.
With carrots for a nose, he grins,
Dancing where the winter begins.

Snowballs fly like fluffy missiles,
While penguins slip in frigid sizzles.
They waddle past with little flair,
On ice skates made of teddy bear.

Laughter echoes in the frosty air,
As kids find snowflakes in their hair.
Hot cocoa spills, a chocolate tide,
While snowmen chuckle, filled with pride.

In frosty air, we twirl and prance,
Where winter whispers, "Take a chance!"
Amidst the chill, our hearts take flight,
In a world where giggles feel just right.

Shivering Serenade

A squirrel dons a knitted cap,
While sliding down a snowy lap.
With acorns tucked in cozy pants,
He shakes his tail and starts to dance.

Bunny hops in fuzzy boots,
As snowflakes swirl like funny loots.
They throw a party, oh so grand,
With peppermint sticks and popcorn strands.

Giggling owls in furry coats,
Sipping tea from tiny oats.
They can't stop laughing at the sight,
Of snowmen planning a snowball fight.

The chilly breeze sings with a grin,
As frosty tales begin to spin.
We'll dance and play until it's night,
In the silly glow of winter's light.

Enchanted Winter Whispers

In the woods, the pine trees sway,
While icicles twinkle in the fray.
A rabbit munches on a snack,
Then bumps into a snowball stack.

Giggles ripple through the chill,
As penguins march with icy will.
They slip and slide, a sight to behold,
With flippers flailing, so bold!

Frosty cheeks and cold, pink noses,
As winter's charm in laughter dozes.
Hot cookies baking, oh so fine,
While marshmallow armies toast and dine.

The snowmen dance, heads bobbing round,
In a snowy world where joy is found.
We'll gather 'round our frosty cheer,
And whisper secrets, crisp and clear.

Crystal Dreams in the Gloom

Underneath a sky so dreary,
A hedgehog spins, oh so merry.
With tiny skates on tiny feet,
He glides and twirls, a snowy treat.

Icicles hanging like a chandelier,
While cuddly bears bring up the rear.
They share a laugh and sips of tea,
Finding joy in winter's spree.

Snowflakes tumble, soft and light,
As turtles join the frosty fight.
With giant smiles, they throw and catch,
A jolly gang without a match.

A friendly fox sings a wintry tune,
Beneath the gaze of a snowy moon.
With laughter echoing like a feast,
We dream of frosts and dance like beasts.

A Pause in the Frozen Air

In a world wrapped tight, like a burrito,
A penguin dances, calls it a 'cheeto.'
Hot cocoa spills, marshmallows take flight,
A snowman sneezes, oh what a sight!

Flakes swirl and twirl, like a party scene,
A squirrel in a scarf, looking quite keen.
The chill in the air tries to make me pout,
But the giggles escape; I can't turn them out!

Icicles hang, like chandeliers cold,
A gingerbread house looking so bold.
With frosting fights and a cookie war,
We laugh till we drop, then laugh even more!

Chasing frostflakes that tickle my nose,
I chase after dreams, where silliness flows.
With every slip on the icy lane,
I tumble through laughter, and dance in the rain!

Silhouettes of Frosty Fantasies

Beneath the moon's gaze, I see quite a show,
A cat wearing boots, strutting through snow.
Suddenly, a snowball, thrown with some glee,
It hits me right square, oh must it be me?

Frosty shapes take form in the night,
A penguin on ice skates, what a delight!
He tumbles and rolls in a snowy embrace,
While rabbits in mittens set quite a pace.

A snowdog with style, sporting a hat,
He joins in the frolic, imagine that!
We waltz through the flakes, invigorated fun,
Chasing shadows 'til day is undone.

With each frosty twinkle in the dark sky,
I seek out the laughter, and giggle nearby.
For in this cold world, with dreams so amusing,
We dive into joy, forever choosing!

Flights of Fancy in Icy Light

Up in the air, on a sled made of whim,
We zoom past the elves, quite close to the brim.
A twirl and a spin, oh watch out for trees,
Laughter erupts, carried on the breeze.

Snowflakes like confetti rain down from above,
While reindeer laugh hard, in fits of pure love.
I craft a big angel, just for the fun,
A snowball surprises - it's never quite done!

The trees wear white coats, all iced up for cheer,
As bunnies do cartwheels, without any fear.
We share silly stories, around fires aglow,
With cocoa in hand, our smiles overflow.

Floating in dreams, we chase pure delight,
Through the frosty landscape, lit bright as the night.
In this world of wonder, everything's right,
Come join the capers, till morning's first light!

The Heart's Chill-Kissed Reverie

With a tiptoe through frost, I'm on a grand quest,
To find the best giggles, where joy feels the best.
The trees sing along, their branches in sway,
While I chase a snowman who thinks he can play!

Marshmallow snowballs fly through the thick air,
A dog in a coat and boots, wags with flair.
The frosty breath puffs, in shapes oh so bright,
As we waddle and tumble in pure, gleeful fright.

With laughter that echoes through chilly blue skies,
Our hearts feel the warmth, as our cheekbones rise.
Each tumble, each fall, a new story unfolds,
In the heart of the winter, a treasure of golds.

A whimsical world where we dance and we dash,
Through snowflakes that sparkle, in a glittery splash.
Embracing the chill, we weave through our play
In this joyous chill, we've found our own way!

The Silent Shimmer of Winter

Flakes dance down like ticklish sprites,
They tumble and roll with giggly bites.
A snowman grins with his carrot nose,
But watch out, he sneezes when he froze!

The trees wear coats of dazzling white,
Challenging squirrels to take flight.
They slip and slide, for goodness sake,
While fashioning snowballs for a sweet break.

Frosty breath makes funny shapes,
A penguin in shorts? How it scrapes!
With frozen toes, I hop and shout,
This chilly circus, no doubt, no doubt!

When the sun peeks through with a smile,
Melting wonders, all the while.
But as puddles form, I have a plan,
To make a boat from an old tin can!

Dreamscapes in White Shrouds

In fluffy clouds, the kittens play,
They tumble down on a snowy tray.
One lands face-first, a sight to see,
Then shakes off snow like a giddy bee!

The world is wrapped in a cozy quilt,
Each branch and gate, a frosty tilt.
But beware the snowball sneaks out late,
They plotted hard to seal my fate!

Cups of cocoa with marshmallow hats,
Quick-frozen giggles and cheeky chats.
We take our sleds and race on down,
The fastest one will wear the crown!

So as the day ends with sparkly glee,
Don't forget your mittens, that's key!
For the real fun starts when we all freeze,
And form a snow angel with the greatest ease!

Moonlit Frost Waltz

Under moonlight, the shadows prance,
As snowflakes twirl in a merry dance.
The penguins wear shoes, oh what a sight,
And lowly snowmen join in, how polite!

The frost bites back with ticklish chills,
While snowballs fly with mischievous thrills.
Laughter echoes through the silent night,
In this winter waltz of pure delight.

Icicles drip like frozen tongues,
Shooting out jokes that we once sung.
Who knew that winter could be so grand,
With giggles and wiggles, hand in hand?

So grab your friends and catch a dream,
In a moonlit world, joy's the theme!
It's a frosty riddle that never ends,
With dancing snowflakes, and laughing friends!

Echoes of Icy Dreams

In fields of white, the secrets hide,
Where snowflakes chuckle and spring a glide.
The rabbits hop, oh what a leap,
Diving nose-first in snow piled deep!

Snowmen gossip about the weather,
As they try to knit a puffy sweater.
With buttons for eyes and smiles so wide,
They tell silly tales, with frosty pride.

Twinkling stars in the chilly air,
Like frozen giggles, beyond compare.
With each sparkle, whispers creep,
Of funny dreams from icy sleep.

So gather 'round for a tale to share,
Of dancing frost and snowflakes rare.
For in this winter wonderland spree,
Laughter surrounds, and you're wild and free!

Hushed Visions on a Frozen Breeze

In a world of frozen fluff,
I built a snowman, a bit too tough.
He wobbled and jiggled, what a sight,
I swear he winked, in sheer delight.

My mittens soaked, my toes a-cold,
I tried to dance, but fell, I'm told.
The snowflakes giggled as I pranced,
In this frosty ballet, I took a chance.

A penguin whispered, with a sly grin,
"You think you'll win? Oh, buddy, just spin!"
I twirled and fell, a frozen ballet,
The laughter echoed, what a silly display.

And when the sun peeked, the snow began to melt,
In our laughing kingdom, joy was felt.
These hilarious frights, I'd never trade,
Here in my laughter, I'm never afraid.

Beneath the Winter's Gaze

Beneath the sky, so deep and gray,
I tripped on ice in a comical way.
My hot cocoa splashed, a chocolate spray,
As giggles erupted, brightening the day.

The squirrels in coats dashed like they owned the park,
I attempted to join, but missed my mark.
With a crash and a boom, the world seemed to stop,
As I landed on snow, a fluffy, soft plop.

The puffy flakes danced, with glee in their flight,
A snowball battle broke out, what a sight!
I threw my best shot, but it flopped in the air,
Laughter erupting, echoing everywhere.

'Tis the season to laugh, to frolic and play,
In this winter wonderland, let joy lead the way.
With every slip and trip, a memory made,
Under winter's gaze, jokes serenely invade.

Translucent Wishes on a Glacial Night

Under the moon, so bright and round,
I made a wish, lost, then found.
A snowman's hat flew up with the breeze,
And landed right on a nearby tree!

The stars chuckled, the owls, they cheered,
As I chased a natty snowball, never feared.
Each toss and each twirl felt merely absurd,
A flurry of giggles, as nonsense occurred.

A snowflake danced, it tickled my nose,
I tried to catch it, but nobody knows.
Then I tripped over a hidden plot,
Fell into fluff, and laughed quite a lot.

In this glacial night, fun reigns supreme,
With popcorn snow and frosty dreams.
So let's make wishes, let laughter ignite,
On this splendidly silly, wintry night.

Whispers of a Frostbitten Heart

Oh, the frost nips gently at my nose,
As I skied downhill clad in beautiful clothes.
With a flip and a flop, I whirled through the air,
And landed straight down in a snow-covered chair.

The trees whispered secrets in soft, hushed tones,
While I flapped my arms like a bird with no bones.
A penguin passed by, gave me a nod,
"Fashionable fall, or just a facade?"

I brushed off my pride, spawned a snowball spree,
And with one little toss, I aimed for a tree.
But the ball ricocheted and hit my own back,
As snickers erupted like a comedy crack.

Yet here amidst laughter, my frostbitten heart,
Knows this wintry playtime is a glorious art.
So bring on the glitter, the fluff, and the cheer,
In this funny old winter, I cherish each year.

Whimsy in Winter's Embrace

A penguin in a top hat, oh my!
He's dancing with snowmen, oh how they fly!
A snowball fight with giggles galore,
Where icicles jingle, and friendships soar.

A squirrel skis down a mound of fluff,
While rabbits in boots try not to bluff.
They tumble and trip, so full of delight,
In this silly wonderland, delightfully bright.

With candy canes as walking sticks,
They navigate through snowy tricks.
A snowflake floats just like a kite,
As laughter echoes into the night.

The trees wear coats of powdered white,
In this frosty world, everything feels right.
With every breath, a frosty sigh,
Winter's whimsy is hard to deny.

Ethereal White Memories

A moose in pajamas, sipping hot cheer,
Tells tales of a wintery deer.
They built a castle with jellybean walls,
Where penguins play tag in snow-dusted halls.

A polar bear with a tutu so bright,
Twirls around under stars at night.
With marshmallow snowflakes falling in fluff,
They're all having fun, but who's had enough?

Chubby snowmen throw snow in the air,
Top hats askew with charming despair.
As frosty friends dance across the white,
Even the owls join in with delight.

In this swirling fluff, with ice on the trees,
Laughter rings out like a winter breeze.
With every snowfall, memories play,
In a realm of white, where we laugh all day.

A Tapestry of Frozen Thoughts

Icicles hanging like silly mustaches,
On rooftops adorned in winter's splashes.
A snow goose sings with croaky delight,
Chasing its tail in a frosty flight.

Gnarled trees dressed in powdery threads,
Holding up banners of snow-white spreads.
Chasing the wind, with mittens askew,
Winter's laughter is bright and true.

The hot cocoa spills on the floor with a splat,
And a cat in a scarf lounges down flat.
While frosted windows frame the jolly scene,
A snowman's hat is far from pristine.

The sky is a quilt of gray and white,
But with giggles aplenty, we bask in its light.
With each chilly breath, a story unfurls,
In this frozen wonderland, joy whirls.

Fragments of Frosted Fancies

A beaver builds a boat of ice and shimmy,
While squirrels throw snowballs—they're a bit gimmicky!

A shivery magpie croons a silly song,
In this snowy realm, where everyone belongs.

Fuzzy mittens chase their friends around,
While snowflakes giggle, never to drown.
With frosty noses, red as a rose,
They bask in winter and whatever it shows.

A cheeky rabbit hops in a sassy hat,
While grinning hedgehogs weave through the spat.
In a flurry of fun, they twirl and spin,
In this blizzard of joy, let the magic begin!

With twinkling lights on trees all a-glow,
They laugh and slide down the ice so slow.
Every moment is crispy yet warm,
In this whimsical land, where dreams take form.

Milton Keynes UK
Ingram Content Group UK Ltd.
UKHW021241191124
451300UK00007B/170

9 789916 944943